To my daughters—one fiery and dramatic,
the other quiet and calm. I love both equally.

—C.A.

To my lovely father, who is like an active
volcano ready to erupt at any moment.

—W.T.

This edition published in 2024 by Flying Eye Books Ltd.
27 Westgate Street, London, E8 3RL

Text © Catherine Ard 2024
Illustrations © Wenjia Tang 2024

Every attempt has been made to ensure any statements written as fact have been checked
to the best of our abilities. However, we are still human, thankfully, and occasionally little
mistakes may crop up. Should you spot any errors, please email info@nobrow.net.

Edited by Sara Forster and Christina Webb
Designed by Ivanna Khomyak
Earth science consultant Dr Rebecca Williams

1 3 5 7 9 10 8 6 4 2

Published by Flying Eye Books Ltd.
Printed in China on FSC® certified paper.

ISBN: 978-1-83874-883-8

FSC
www.fsc.org

MIX
Paper | Supporting
responsible forestry
FSC® C137217

www.flyingeyebooks.com

Catherine Ard • Wenjia Tang

INTO THE VOLCANO

The Science, Magic, and Meaning of Volcanoes

Flying Eye Books

Contents

LIVING WITH VOLCANOES

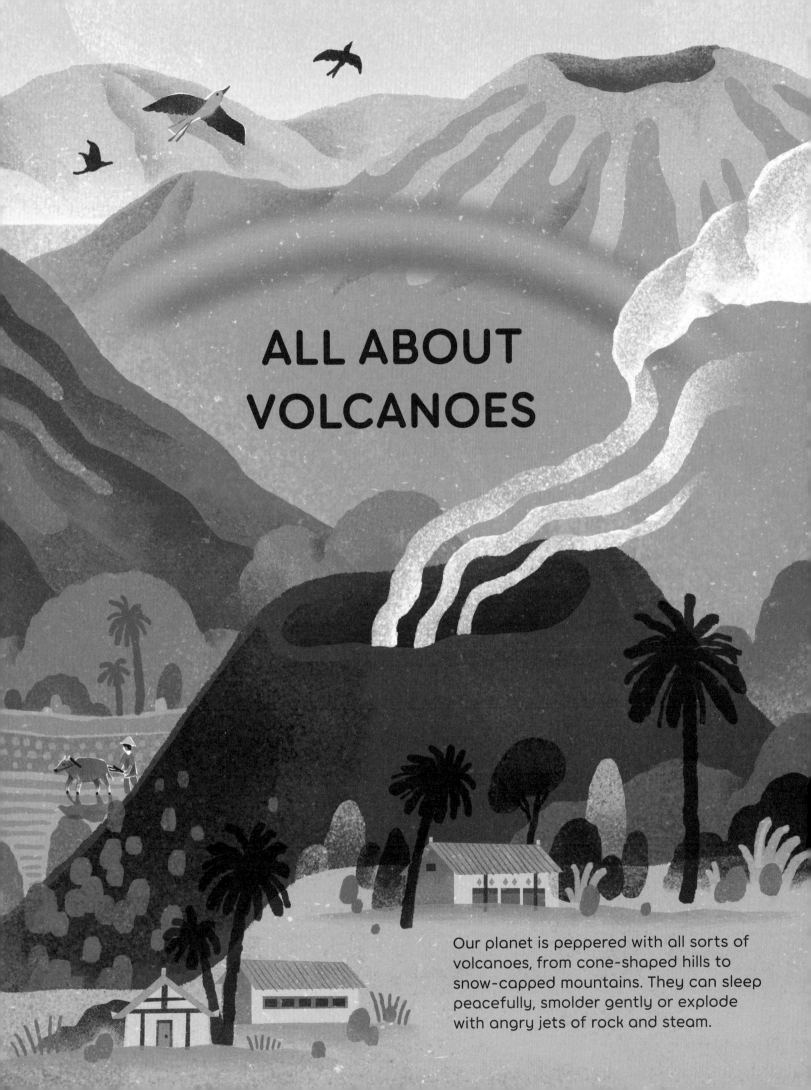

ALL ABOUT VOLCANOES

Our planet is peppered with all sorts of volcanoes, from cone-shaped hills to snow-capped mountains. They can sleep peacefully, smolder gently or explode with angry jets of rock and steam.

Going Underground

The ground you walk on feels completely solid, but deep below your feet there are huge magma chambers containing pockets of molten rock. When this escapes through a hole in the Earth's surface, a volcano is formed.

Inside the Earth

If you cut our planet in half, you would see its different layers.

Crust

This is the cool, rocky surface of the Earth that we live on.

Mantle

Under the crust lies a layer of very hot rock called the mantle. This layer is mostly solid but some parts can move slowly like sticky liquid.

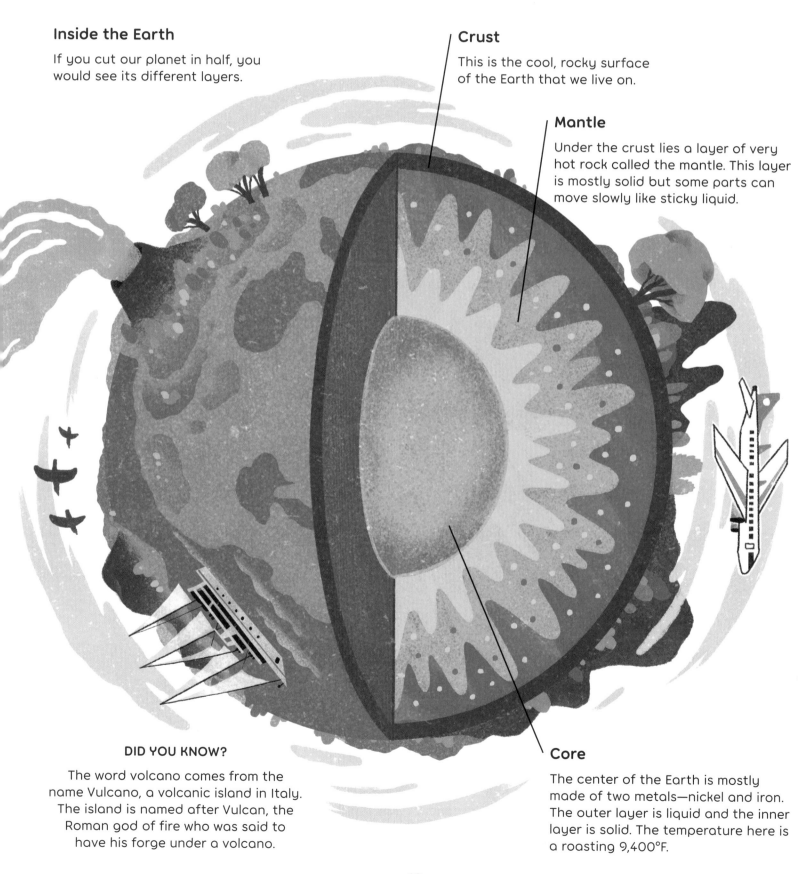

DID YOU KNOW?

The word volcano comes from the name Vulcano, a volcanic island in Italy. The island is named after Vulcan, the Roman god of fire who was said to have his forge under a volcano.

Core

The center of the Earth is mostly made of two metals—nickel and iron. The outer layer is liquid and the inner layer is solid. The temperature here is a roasting 9,400°F.

Our giant jigsaw

Earth's crust is made up of huge slabs of rock that fit together like a jigsaw puzzle. The pieces are called tectonic plates. They move very slowly in different directions. Where the edges of plates meet, volcanoes can form.

Clash

When two plates bump together or converge, one plate slides under the other. The bottom plate causes melting in the mantle, creating hot, liquid rock.

Separate

Some plates pull apart or diverge, leaving a space in the Earth's crust. This is filled by hot rock from below, which melts as it rises.

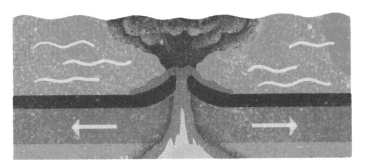

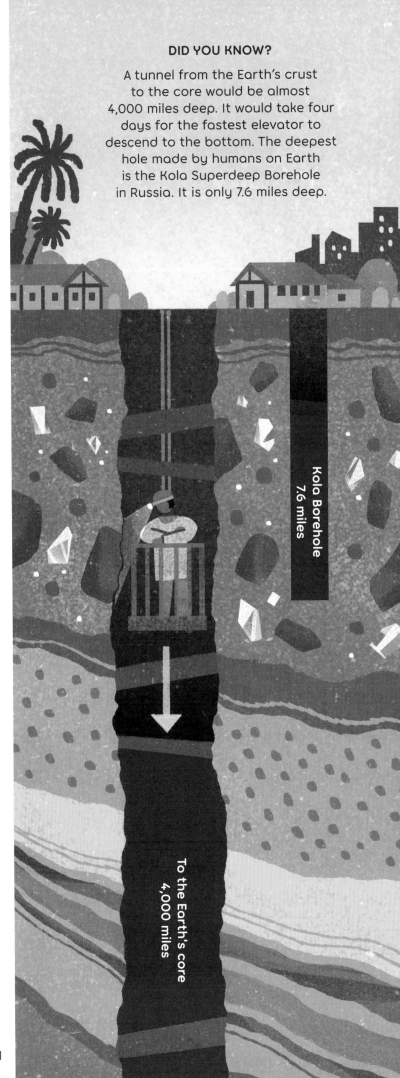

A tunnel from the Earth's crust to the core would be almost 4,000 miles deep. It would take four days for the fastest elevator to descend to the bottom. The deepest hole made by humans on Earth is the Kola Superdeep Borehole in Russia. It is only 7.6 miles deep.

Kola Borehole
7.6 miles

To the Earth's core
4,000 miles

Volcanoes Today

There are more than 1,500 active volcanoes in the world. Some have not erupted for hundreds of years, while others erupt almost constantly. About twenty volcanoes are erupting as you read this!

Sleeping giant

Mount Fuji in Japan has not erupted for over 300 years, but some experts believe it could be building up for an eruption soon.

Big bang

In 1980, Mount St Helens in the USA began to stir after 100 years. No one predicted the shattering blast that followed. It was the most deadly eruption the country had ever known.

Eurasian plate

North American plate

NORTH AMERICA

Mount Fuji

ASIA

Mount St Helens

The Ring of Fire

Most active volcanoes are found in a long, horseshoe-shaped chain called the Ring of Fire, that stretches for over 25,000 miles. It contains an incredible 452 volcanoes, including some of the most powerful in the world.

Popocatepetl

Nevado del Ruiz

Cotopaxi

La Cumbre

Krakatau   Mount Bromo

SOUTH AMERICA

AUSTRALIA

Pacific plate

Australian plate

South American plate

Little and often

Kīlauea, in Hawaii, erupted almost continuously from 1983 to 2018. Italy's Mount Etna has been almost constantly active in the last ten years!

Katla

Eurasian plate

EUROPE

Vesuvius

Mount Etna

ASIA

Indian plate

AFRICA

Erta Ale

Ol Doinyo
Lengai

African plate

Antarctic plate

Ring of Fire

Tectonic plates

Volcanoes

Eruption

A volcano is erupting. The ground shudders and a thundering rumble can be heard for miles around. Tiny particles of rock, called volcanic ash, fill the air, and the top of the mountain glows.

Underground, hot melted rock called magma rises up through a gap in the Earth's crust. The magma is full of bubbling gases and steam. It builds up in a chamber beneath the volcano. When the pressure builds up in the chamber, magma is forced up through a hole called a vent. Finally, it bursts out of the opening at the top. When magma flows out, the orange rock is called lava. It can also explode out as a thick cloud of boiling gas, steam and ash.

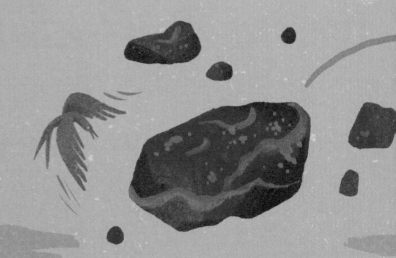

LOOK OUT!

Big blobs of lava cool in mid-air to form lava bombs. Some are as big as a cars!

Lava flow

DID YOU KNOW?

An ash cloud from an erupting volcano can reach up to 38 miles into the air. It is filled with deadly gases.

Ash cloud

Crater

CRACK!
Ash rubs together in
the air to make bolts
of lightning.

Magma

Vent

Magma chamber

A Long Life

A volcano is like a living thing. It emerges one day, grows over time, gets old and eventually falls asleep or dies. Grassy hills, peaceful lakes and even castles could be volcanoes of the past in disguise!

Active

An active volcano is one that has erupted at least once in the last 10,000 years. It may be erupting now or be ready to erupt at any time.

Mount Etna in Italy is one of the world's most active volcanoes. It has regular explosions and lava flows.

Dormant

Volcanoes can lie sleeping for thousands of years and then wake up. A dormant volcano is one that is not currently erupting but might in the future.

Crater lake in Oregon, USA sits on top of Mount Mazama, a dormant volcano that last erupted over 4,000 years ago.

Edinburgh Castle in Scotland was built on the remains of an extinct volcano.

Extinct

This is a volcano that has not erupted for at least 10,000 years. The magma chamber is empty and it will probably never come back to life, but you never know . . .

All Shapes and Sizes

Some volcanoes are steep and tall, but many are gently sloping and small. Some volcanoes erupt quietly, while others blow their tops. What forms above ground all depends on what is happening down below.

Way to blow!

The type of magma and the bubbles of gas trapped inside cause volcanoes to erupt in different ways.

Explosive Eruptions

Thick magma traps bubbles of gas inside it. Pressure builds as the gas-filled magma is forced up the narrow neck of the volcano. Finally, it explodes out of the top—like fizzy drink from a shaken bottle. The sticky lava does not flow far before it hardens, creating volcanoes with steep sides.

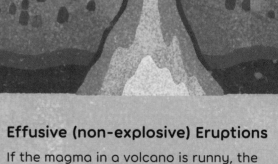

Effusive (non-explosive) Eruptions

If the magma in a volcano is runny, the bubbles of gas can escape easily. The lava oozes out and travels a long way before it cools, making gently sloping sides.

Scoria cone

These small volcanoes blow out tiny pieces of lava, called scoria. The scoria cools and falls around the vent to form a cone shape. Scoria cones often form on the sides of larger volcanoes.

Stratovolcano

These volcanoes erupt violently, throwing out large amounts of lava, rock and ash which build up to form steep sides.

Caldera

When a stratovolcano has a huge eruption, the walls and the bottom of the volcano can collapse, leaving a giant bowl-shaped hole called a crater. The crater is often filled with a lake.

Shield volcanoes

These wide volcanoes have sloping sides that make them look like a warrior's shield. They are made of layer upon layer of runny lava that flows down their slopes.

Meet the Experts

Imagine hiking up an erupting volcano, walking over smoking-hot ground and peering into a lake of bubbling lava with deafening sounds all around. It's all in a day's work for a volcanologist!

Predicting Eruptions

A volcanologist is a scientist who studies volcanoes. It is one of the most dangerous jobs in the world. They spend time on active volcanoes taking pictures and measurements and gathering samples of red-hot lava to help understand when volcanoes might erupt. This allows people who live nearby to get to safety in time.

Looking for clues

Thermometers and chemical sensors are used to monitor the temperature and the amount of gas in the air. If these things start to increase, it means an eruption could happen soon.

The ground around a volcano shakes for a few weeks before an eruption. A seismometer records the vibrations.

When magma starts to build under a volcano, the ground can bulge and swell. A tiltmeter measures tiny changes in the slope of the ground.

Safe research

Remote-controlled robots and drones gather information from parts of volcanoes that are too dangerous for humans to visit. Satellites can even monitor volcanoes from space!

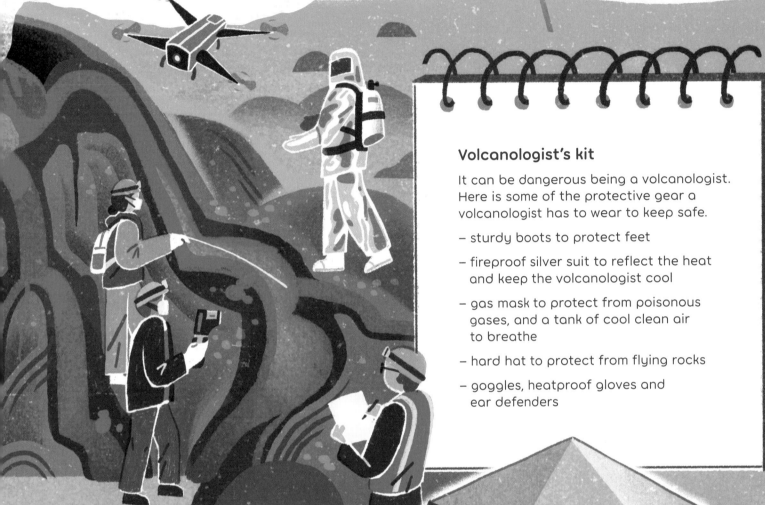

Volcanologist's kit

It can be dangerous being a volcanologist. Here is some of the protective gear a volcanologist has to wear to keep safe.

- sturdy boots to protect feet

- fireproof silver suit to reflect the heat and keep the volcanologist cool

- gas mask to protect from poisonous gases, and a tank of cool clean air to breathe

- hard hat to protect from flying rocks

- goggles, heatproof gloves and ear defenders

Daring duo

Fearless French volcanologists Katia and Maurice Krafft traveled the world to get up close to erupting volcanoes. Their work helped scientists understand more about eruptions and made people more aware of the dangers. Tragically, the couple were killed when Mount Unzen in Japan erupted in 1991.

DID YOU KNOW?

Around 60 volcanoes erupt every year and as many as 20 could be erupting each day. That's a lot of work for volcanologists to do.

VOLCANOES EVERYWHERE

If you happened to be gazing at this spot off the coast of Iceland on the 14th of November 1963, you would have spotted an ash plume rising from the sea. A day later, land appeared. The island grew over a few years and it was named Surtsey, after the Norse god of fire.

Underwater Volcanoes

Most volcanic eruptions on Earth go unseen, on the ocean floor. Underwater volcanoes are called seamounts. Sometimes the tip of a seamount reaches the surface and a new island is born.

Making new islands

There could be as many as a million seamounts under the sea. This is because the Earth's crust is thinner under the ocean.

1. When molten rock breaks through onto the seabed, it flows slowly and is cooled quickly by the seawater.

2. After many eruptions, lava piles up and a cone shape forms.

3. When the lava reaches the surface, a new island is created.

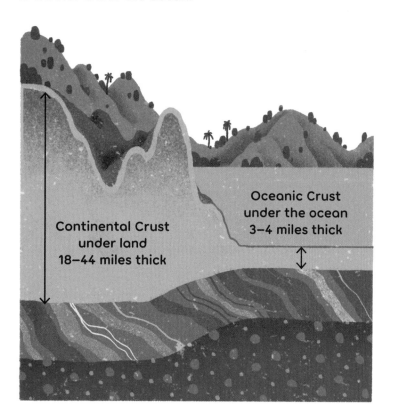

Continental Crust under land 18–44 miles thick

Oceanic Crust under the ocean 3–4 miles thick

Disappearing islands

Some new islands are worn away by the waves before they are added to a map. Others disappear over thousands of years as the volcano that formed them sinks back into the sea.

Deep-sea smokers

Down in the dark, ice-cold ocean, clouds of boiling seawater billow from chimneys on the seabed. These are hydrothermal vents which form when seawater seeps through cracks in the ocean floor. It is superheated by magma and blasted back out, bringing chemicals with it.

Vulcanoctopus

Scaly-foot snail

Giant tube worms

Pink vent fish

Shrimp

Yeti crab

Giant vent mussels

Squat lobster

Hot water home

Scientists use remote-controlled robots to explore the ocean floor. They have found some unusual creatures thriving in these hostile hotspots. Vents are crowded with crabs, tube worms, mussels and shrimp despite the toxic chemicals and scalding water.

25

The planets and moons in our Solar System have volcanoes, too. Many have not erupted for millions of years, but some are still gushing tons of lava and gas.

Secret eruptions

Venus has over 1,000 volcanoes—more than anywhere else in the Solar System. It is not known exactly how many are active, as they are hidden below thick clouds of gas that cover the planet's surface.

Mon-strous

The largest known volcano in the Solar System is Olympus Mons on Mars. At 16 miles high it is three times taller than Everest, Earth's tallest mountain.

Moon rock

When astronauts brought samples of rock back from the Moon, scientists discovered that it was actually cooled lava. This means that the Moon was once volcanically active!

Record breaker

The most impressive volcanoes in the Solar System are found on one of Jupiter's moons. Io (pronounced Eye-oh) has over 160 active volcanoes. Some of its craters are bigger than Earth's major cities.

Blast off!

Io is home to the most powerful volcano in the Solar System, Loki Patera. Eruptions can blast lava and gas hundreds of miles high.

DID YOU KNOW?

Astronomers study space volcanoes using huge telescopes on Earth and uncrewed spacecrafts, called probes.

Unusual Volcanoes

When heat, gases and water mix underground they create a range of strange eruptions on the surface.

Slurp, pop!

That is the sound of a gloopy mud volcano. They form when underground gases and water mix and dissolve the surrounding rock. Mud "lava" is usually cool—it is the gases in the mud that make it bubble. Large mud volcanoes are popular places to sink into a soothing mud bath.

Fire and ice

In the cold North and South Poles, volcanoes erupt under glaciers. Magma melts the covering of snow and ice, then the water mixes with lava to create towering clouds of steam and ash.

Letting off steam

In some volcanic areas, magma heats up underground water. It escapes on the surface as bubbling hot springs, jets of steam called fumaroles, and geysers that shoot columns of hot water into the air at regular intervals.

DID YOU KNOW?

In 2010, a volcano erupted under a glacier in Iceland. It created an ash cloud so big it spread across most of Europe. Ash particles clog up jet engines, so thousands of flights had to be canceled.

STORIES, MYTHS AND LEGENDS

Volcanoes have inspired stories that have been passed down for thousands of years. The Aboriginal people of South Australia tell of a giant creature with teeth made of lava. This was probably the Budj Bim volcano that last erupted 37,000 years ago!

A City Beneath the Waves

There is a famous Greek myth about Atlantis, a paradise island that sank below the sea. It is a story that has fascinated the world for thousands of years, and people are still searching for the legendary lost city today.

Island life

Legend says that Atlantis was a powerful empire based on a paradise island full of rare and exotic wildlife. People grew plenty of food and kept animals. They also built a great city and had silver, gold, and wealth beyond their dreams. Life was perfect.

Enough is enough

Even though they had everything they could wish for, the people of Atlantis became greedy and dishonest. They stopped respecting the gods and worshipped wealth and possessions instead. Zeus, the king of all Greek gods, grew angry when he saw this. He sent violent volcanoes and earthquakes. Overnight, Atlantis was swallowed up by the sea.

True or false?

Some say the myth is just a moral about being happy with what you have. Others believe it could be based on a real event. Over 3,000 years ago, a massive eruption on the volcanic island of Santorini, near Greece, sank half the island and destroyed an entire civilization. It was probably one of the largest volcanic events in the planet's history. Could it have been Atlantis?

The Sorceress

Iceland is known as "the land of fire and ice." Glittering glaciers and frozen waterfalls sit alongside hot springs and smoking volcanoes. Katla is one of the largest and most active volcanoes.

Katla the sorceress

A tale is told of a monastery nestled among the hills near the Mýrdalsjökull glacier. The monastery thrived, with villagers working together to survive the harsh winters. Among them was the housekeeper, Katla, a woman who was feared for her hot temper and special powers. It was whispered that she was an evil sorceress.

Magic trousers

Katla owned a magical pair of pants. Whoever wore them could run as fast as the wind and never get tired. One day, a shepherd needed to round up his sheep before a thunderstorm broke. He thought of Katla and her magic pants and ran to her for help. She was not home, but the shepherd spotted her magic pants and put them on. He ran like the wind, rounded up his flock and replaced the pants without being discovered.

DID YOU KNOW?

Katla means "kettle" or "cauldron" in Icelandic. As well as being the name of the volcano, it is one of the most popular girls' names in Iceland.

Red-hot rage

When Katla returned, she knew instantly what had happened. In a rage, she lured the shepherd down to the monastery's wine cellar where she drowned him in a vat of wine. Fearing discovery, Katla ran away. She jumped into a crack in the glacier and landed in a sleeping volcano beneath the ice. Shortly after, there was a huge glacial flood that destroyed everything for miles around, including the monastery. Since that day, the volcano has been known as Katla.

Goddess of Volcanoes

The American state of Hawaii is a string of islands in the Pacific Ocean. They were created by volcanoes that erupted from the seabed—but there are many stories about how the fiery islands came to be.

A fiery temper

Pele, the Hawaiian goddess of volcanoes and fire, is said to have created the islands. She had a hot temper that made her both honored and feared. She could cause earthquakes by stamping her feet and bring on eruptions by digging with her magic stick.

Legend says that Pele sometimes warns locals of an eruption before it happens. She walks the streets near the volcano of Kīlauea disguised either as a beautiful young woman or an old woman with white hair. Anyone who sees her must pass on the warning or they will suffer in the next eruption.

DID YOU KNOW?

Golden glass strands that sometimes form when lava cools are called Pele's hair. Jet black droplets of volcanic glass are called Pele's tears.

The Creation Story

Over 700 years ago, the Māori people traveled from Polynesia to New Zealand in canoes. They found their new home to be one of shaking ground, steaming pools and fiery mountains. The Māori told stories to explain these strange things.

How it all began

In the beginning, Ranginui (the sky father) and Papatūānuku (the mother earth) were joined together in an eternal hug and their sons were born between them in darkness. Their children wanted light and warmth, so they decided to separate their parents to allow light to come into the world.

Ruaumoko, God of Volcanoes

After the parents were forced apart, Ranginui cried, and his tears rained down from the sky onto the land. To stop this, the children decided to turn Papatūānuku face-down, so the parents could no longer see each other's sorrow. Rūaumoko, the youngest son, was still at his mother's breast when this happened, so he was carried into the world below. His movements under the ground cause earthquakes and volcanoes.

DID YOU KNOW?

One of Jupiter's moons, Io, has many volcanic craters, called paterae. One is named Rūaumoko Patera after the Māori god of volcanoes.

A Mexican Love Story

On a clear day in Mexico City, two volcanoes can be seen in the distance. They are Popocatépetl and Iztaccíhuatl, or Izta and Popo, as they are known by locals. They are a symbol of a love that will never die.

Rival tribes

Izta was a princess of the Tlaxcalan tribe. Her father wanted her to marry a Tlaxcala prince but she was in love with Popo, a prince from the rival Chichimeca tribe. Izta's father finally agreed to let Popo marry his daughter on the condition that he fight alongside the Tlaxcalans to defeat the Aztecs, who were their enemies.

Broken hearts

While Popo was away at war, one of Izta's jealous suitors, Citlaltepetl, lied and told her that Popocatepetl had died in battle. Iztaccíhuatl was inconsolable and cried until her heart stopped.

When he returned from battle, Popo found his beloved Izta dead. The grief-stricken prince built an enormous tomb and carried Izta to the top. He knelt down beside her body and promised to watch over her with a burning torch until she woke up.

Eternal love

Centuries passed and the pair were covered with snow and earth until they became the volcanoes they are today, with Itza in the shape of a woman lying down and Popo a kneeling man. Legend has it that Popo still watches over Izta. That is why the Popo volcano continues to smoke, while the other volcano next to it is dormant. Popo's pain still burns so deep within his heart that occasionally the volcano erupts.

DID YOU KNOW?

The name Popocatépetl means "Smoking Mountain" in ancient Aztec language. It has erupted 15 times in the last 500 years.

41

VOLCANOES IN THE ARTS

In Jules Verne's novel *Journey to the Center of the Earth* three explorers descend into the Earth through a crater in an Icelandic volcano. After sailing on an underground ocean and battling prehistoric creatures they are blown back to the surface by the Italian volcano Stromboli.

Villains and Volcanoes

Menacing volcanoes often go hand-in-hand with the evil characters in books and films. In the film *You Only Live Twice*, the villain Blofeld has his secret lair inside a volcano and in the Disney animation *Moana*, Te Kā is a destructive Polynesian goddess made of lava.

The Lord of the Rings

In the fantasy novel by J.R.R.Tolkien, a black volcanic land called Mordor is ruled by the evil Sauron. A foreboding volcano called Mount Doom lies right at Mordor's center. The hero, Frodo Baggins, must defeat Sauron and destroy the enchanted Ring by throwing it into the volcano's fiery crater.

Frankenstein

This famous horror story may never have been written if it was not for a volcanic eruption. In 1815, ash from Mount Tambora in Indonesia blocked the sun and the world was plunged into a "volcanic winter" in 1816. *Frankenstein*'s author, Mary Shelley, spent a summer with friends sheltering from the rain. To pass the time, they competed to see who could write the best ghost story. Shelley won with her tale about a hideous monster made from old body parts.

DID YOU KNOW?

The Mount Tomboro eruption lowered world temperatures by 5.4°F. In Europe and North America, 1816 became known as "The Year Without a Summer."

Explosive Art

For centuries, volcanoes have been a favorite subject for artists. Paintings of eruptions full of drama and color and looming snow-capped peaks show how our planet can be both beautiful or threatening—or both at once.

Inspiring eruption

British artist Joseph Wright (1734–1797) was inspired by his visit to Vesuvius, Italy, in the 1770s and painted over 30 views of the volcano. In *Vesuvius in Eruption, with a View over the Islands in the Bay of Naples* the artist contrasts the dramatic explosion with the calm sea and the cool moonlight.

Perfect peak

Japanese artist Hokusai (1760–1849) made over 100 prints of Mount Fuji, Japan's highest mountain. Hokusai's pictures show the volcano from different locations, in different seasons and weather. *The Great Wave off Kanagawa* is famous throughout the world.

Nature's pain

During the autumn of 1883 or the winter of 1884, Norwegian painter Edvard Munch (1863-1944) stood in Oslo looking at a blood-red sunset. He said he felt "a great, unending scream piercing through nature," and this inspired his world-famous painting *The Scream*.

Scientists believe Munch was probably witnessing the effects of a volcanic eruption over 10,000 miles away. Krakatau exploded in Indonesia on August 27, 1883 sending dust and gases miles into the sky.

Folk art

The Kichwa people of Tigua, Ecuador, farm the slopes and valleys of the Andes mountains. They create colorful art using chicken feather brushes and sheepskin canvases. Their work celebrates festivals, traditions, and their way of life herding sheep and llamas and growing crops. The volcano Cotopaxi is shown in many of their paintings as it such an important part of their culture.

DID YOU KNOW?

Cotopaxi is the third-highest active volcano in the world. It is known to have erupted 87 times. The last time was in 2015.

Making Music

Stradivarius violins are the most expensive musical instruments in the world because of their wonderful sound. For decades scientists have tried to discover their secret. Now it seems that volcanoes from the distant past may be responsible for beautiful music in the present . . .

A master craftsman

Antonio Stradivari was an Italian craftsman who made violins and other string instruments. He worked during a time known as the Little Ice Age, from 1645 to 1715. Conditions throughout the world were much cooler, and winters in Europe were much longer and colder than before.

The Little Ice Age

Scientists think that the Little Ice Age was triggered by four explosive volcanic eruptions between 1250 and 1300, which blasted huge clouds of ash particles into the air. The particles would have reflected the sun's energy back into space. It is thought that the cooling effect from these volcanoes was enough to increase the size of ice sheets around the Arctic Ocean. The extra ice reflected more of the sun's rays back into space and made the planet colder still.

Slow growing

The lack of warm sunshine meant that the trees in Europe grew more slowly. This included the spruce and maple used for the front and back of violins made by Stradivari. It is thought that the slow growth made the wood more even and dense—and helped to produce the pure and wonderful sound.

DID YOU KNOW?

Stradivari made 1,116 instruments. There are only about 650 of them left in the world. The Messiah Stradivarius violin is worth $20 million!

LIVING WITH VOLCANOES

In 2021, for the first time in almost 6,000 years, lava started to spill from Fagradalsfjall in Iceland. Thousands of people hiked across the ice to enjoy the spectacle. They watched in awe, took photos, and even toasted marshmallows on the molten rock.

Blasts from the Past

Since the beginning of life on Earth, volcanoes have caused massive destruction. An eruption can trigger hazards that endanger people, animals, and places both near and far. Some eruptions are so huge and so deadly they will never be forgotten. Like Vesuvius 2,000 years ago . . .

Warning signs

Records from the summer of 79CE report strange happenings around Mount Vesuvius in Italy. There were small earthquakes, dead fish were seen floating in the river, springs dried up, and vines wilted on the mountain slopes. Vesuvius had not erupted for nearly 900 years, so the locals were not alarmed. Today, we would recognize the signs of moving magma and poisonous gases as the volcano got ready to explode.

Huge eruption

On the evening of 24th August 79CE, Mount Vesuvius suddenly erupted. The earth trembled, there was a terrible darkness, and ash and rocks rained down. People had left it too late to escape. In just a few hours the seaside town of Herculaneum was burned to the ground and the city of Pompeii was completely buried.

Fast and furious

The eruption of Vesuvius caused one of the most dangerous hazards of all—a pyroclastic flow. This is a tumbling cloud of poisonous gases, scorching ash, and rock that races downhill at speeds of over 60 miles an hour. It smothers and burns everything in its path.

Frozen in time

Pompeii lay undiscovered for well over a thousand years, then archeologists began to dig down through the thick layers of ash. They uncovered streets, buildings, everyday objects, and artworks as well as the remains of the people who died. These finds have taught us a lot about life in Roman times.

DID YOU KNOW?

Archeologists have made plaster molds of many of the people who died in Pompeii. The shapes of their bodies were preserved in the layers of ash.

Gifts from Underground

Volcanoes are destructive but they can be very useful, too. Millions of people across the world live and work near to volcanoes because of the good things that they bring.

Top crops

After an eruption, volcanic ash smothers plants but ash is also full of nutrients. Over time the nutrients seep into the ground and make rich soil for growing crops. Mount Etna in Sicily, Italy is the most active volcano in Europe but farmers still choose to grow vegetables and grapes on its slopes.

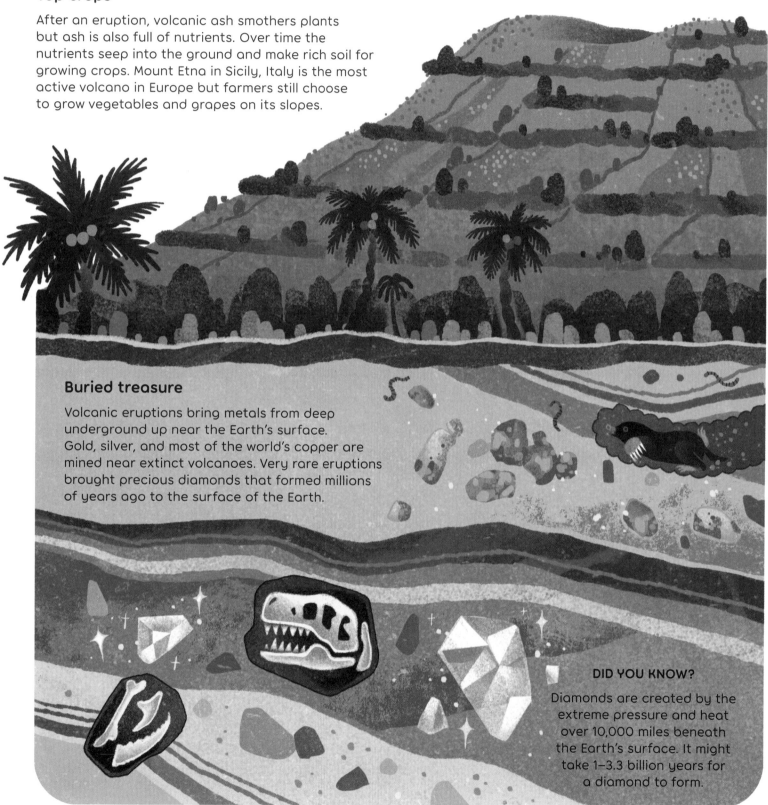

Buried treasure

Volcanic eruptions bring metals from deep underground up near the Earth's surface. Gold, silver, and most of the world's copper are mined near extinct volcanoes. Very rare eruptions brought precious diamonds that formed millions of years ago to the surface of the Earth.

DID YOU KNOW?

Diamonds are created by the extreme pressure and heat over 10,000 miles beneath the Earth's surface. It might take 1–3.3 billion years for a diamond to form.

Green energy

In countries with a lot of volcanic activity, there is an endless supply of clean power, called geothermal energy. Huge pools of underground water are heated naturally by hot rock near to volcanoes. The steam from the water is drawn up to a power plant at the surface and used to generate electricity that is then used to heat homes and greenhouses.

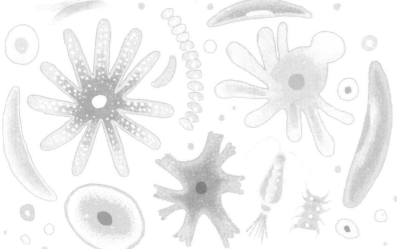

Ocean life

On land, lava destroys everything in its path, but in the ocean, it helps life to thrive. Lava releases nutrients into the water which encourage microscopic plants, called phytoplankton, to grow. Phytoplankton are good because they absorb carbon dioxide—one of the gases that is heating up the planet and causing climate change. They are also eaten by tiny ocean creatures, which in turn feed bigger fish.

Hot Homes

Most animals stay clear of volcanoes, but a few have learned to make the most of the homes, heat, and food that they offer.

Flamingo paradise

It may look tempting, but the shallow water of Lake Natron in Tanzania is burning hot. It sits near to Ol Doinyo Lengai, one of Africa's most active volcanoes, and is fed by bubbling volcanic springs. Most animals cannot survive here but millions of lesser flamingos flock to the lake. Their tough skin and scaly legs prevent burns so they can enjoy eating the bacteria found in the hot water in peace.

Spa monkeys

In the mountains of northern Japan, a group of snow monkeys have discovered a clever way to beat the cold. Every day in winter they come to relax in the steaming, volcanic springs.

Buried birds

Maleo birds of Indonesia lay huge eggs that are too big for the female to sit on, so they bury them in the warm soil near volcanoes. The young birds dig their way out and are able to fly as soon as they hatch!

Warm eggs

Every year, nearly 2,000 land iguanas in the Galápagos make the long journey from the coast to the top of La Cumbre volcano. They clamber down into the crater to lay their eggs in the warm volcanic ash. It is the perfect temperature for their young to develop and hatch.

DID YOU KNOW?

Galápagos iguanas are able to sense volcanic activity before an eruption happens. This gives them time to scurry to safety.

Neat nests

Millions of crested auklet birds gather on Alaska's Aleutian Islands. They nest in the nooks and crannies created by cooled lava. Over time the nesting holes fill up with grass that grows in the birds' poop. An eruption is needed every few years to create fresh nesting sites.

Crater creatures

An extinct volcano in Papua New Guinea is a haven for rare wildlife. Mount Bosavi's huge crater is protected by rocky walls over half a mile high. Inside is a rainforest where scientists discovered 16 new kinds of frog and a giant rat the size of a cat.

Respect for Nature

For many communities who live in the shadow of a volcano, it shapes their lives and their beliefs. Volcanoes, or the powers that control them, have the ability to provide good things or to take them away.

Mount Bromo

Mount Bromo on the island of Java is one of Indonesia's most sacred places. According to an old legend, princess Roro and her husband Joko who ruled the region were unable to have children. They made a deal with the gods where they were given many children, but in exchange their last born had to be offered to the volcano as a sacrifice.

Giving thanks

Today the Tenggerese people who live around Mount Bromo come together for the annual Kasada Ceremony in a temple at the foot of the mountain. On the fourteenth day of the ritual they climb the volcano with flowers, fruit, vegetables, and money for the gods. They throw their offerings into the crater as thanks for the good health and good life that they have been given.

DID YOU KNOW?

Mount Bromo is one of the most active volcanoes in Indonesia. It has erupted more than 55 times since 1804.

Snow-capped symbol

Mount Fuji is the symbol of Japan, and climbing it is one of Japan's most sacred traditions. Every year, around 400,000 hikers snake up its ashy slopes. In Buddhist religion, mountains are seen as ideal places to meditate. You can leave the everyday world behind, and find enlightenment (perfect knowledge and wisdom). Today, not everyone climbs Mount Fuji for religious reasons, but this mountain still has the power to inspire people.

DID YOU KNOW?

"Goraiko" is a special Japanese word for the uplifting feeling you get when you see the sunrise from Mount Fuji.

Glossary

Aboriginal – the first native people of a land

Archeologist – someone who studies human history

Ash plume – a large cloud of ash

Astronomer – someone who studies the Sun, Moon, planets, and stars

Caldera – a volcanic feature formed by the collapse of land surface after a gigantic volcanic eruption

Ceremony – formal actions carried out at an important occasion

Climate change – long-term changes in temperatures and weather patterns

Drone – a flying robot that can be remotely controlled

Fumarole – an opening in or near a volcano, through which hot gases emerge

Geothermal energy – heat that comes from inside the Earth that is used to generate energy

Geyser – a natural spring that shoots up columns of hot water

Glacier – a mass of ice moving slowly along a valley

Nutrient – a substance that is needed to keep a plant or animal alive and to help it grow

Phytoplankton – microscopic plants that live in the ocean

Index

Prehistoric – belonging to a very long time ago, before written records were kept

Pyroclastic flow – a fast moving flow of volcanic ash, rocks, and hot gases

Ritual – a regular ceremony or series of actions

Sacred – to do with a god

Sacrifice – giving up something that you value so that something good may happen

Scalding – very hot liquid or steam

Scoria – rocks formed by the cooling and solidification of molten earth material

Seamount – an underwater mountain

Seismometer – an instrument that measures movement of the ground

Solar System – the Sun and the planets that revolve around it

Tectonic plates – large pieces of the Earth's crust

Thermometer – a device for measuring temperature

Tiltmeter – an instrument that measures the tilt of the Earth's surface

Toxic – something poisonous

Tradition – a custom or belief passed on from one generation to the next

Volcanologist – a scientist who studies volcanoes

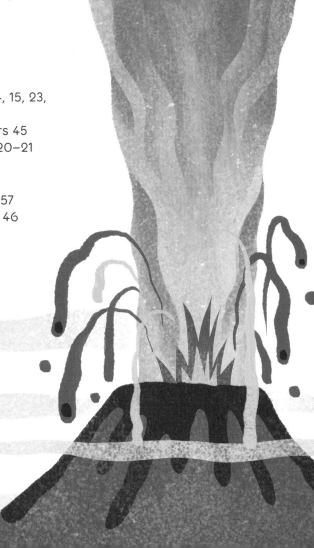